NEWSMAKERS

KATE MIDDLETON
PRINCESS OF WALES

BY MARIE-THERESE MILLER, PHD

Cover image: In May 2023, Kate Middleton attended an event at the Foundling Museum, where she met with foster and adoptive parents to learn about their experiences.

Core Library
An Imprint of Abdo Publishing
abdobooks.com

abdobooks.com

Published by Abdo Publishing, a division of ABDO, PO Box 398166, Minneapolis, Minnesota 55439.

Printed in the United States of America, North Mankato, Minnesota.
102024
012025

THIS BOOK CONTAINS RECYCLED MATERIALS

Cover Photo: Max Mumby/Indigo/Getty Images
Interior Photos: Chris Jackson/Chris Jackson Collection/Getty Images, 4–5; James Devaney/FilmMagic/Getty Images, 9, 43; John Stillwell-WPA Pool/Getty Images Entertainment/Getty Images, 10; Shutterstock Images, 12–13, 17, 36; St Andrew's School-WPA Pool/Getty Images Entertainment/Getty Images, 16; RDImages/Epics/Hulton Archive/Getty Images, 20–21; Graham Barclay/BWP Media/Getty Images News/Getty Images, 22; Handout/Getty Images Publicity/Getty Images, 26; Anwar Hussein Collection/ROTA/WireImage/Getty Images, 28–29; Max Mumby/Indigo/Getty Images, 32, 45; Samir Hussein/WireImage/Getty Images, 34–35; Jonathan Brady/Getty Images Entertainment/Getty Images, 38; Rob Newell/CameraSport/Getty Images, 40

Editor: Kari Cornell
Series Designer: Marley Richmond

Library of Congress Control Number: 2024938370

Publisher's Cataloging-in-Publication Data

Names: Miller, Marie-Therese, author.
Title: Kate Middleton: Princess of Wales / by Marie-Therese Miller
Other title: Princess of Wales
Description: Minneapolis, Minnesota: ABDO Publishing, 2025 | Series: Newsmakers | Includes online resources and index.
Identifiers: ISBN 9781098295707 (lib. bdg.) | ISBN 9798384916703 (ebook)
Subjects: LCSH: Middleton, Kate, 1982---Juvenile literature. | Catherine, Princess of Wales, 1982- --Juvenile literature. | Princesses--Biography--Juvenile literature. | Royalty--Biography--Juvenile literature. | Great Britain--Princes and princesses—Biography--Juvenile literature. | United Kingdom--Juvenile literature.
Classification: DDC 941.086--dc23

CONTENTS

CHAPTER ONE

CATHERINE, DUCHESS OF CAMBRIDGE

It was April 29, 2011. Catherine Elizabeth "Kate" Middleton arrived at Westminster Abbey in London, the United Kingdom. She rode in a Rolls Royce Phantom VI, accompanied by her father, Michael Middleton. It was the day of her wedding to Prince William, Duke of Cambridge. She stepped out of the limousine to cheers and applause from the huge crowd.

Kate wore a timeless wedding gown made of white and ivory satin. English fashion

Kate Middleton was the first commoner to marry into the royal family since 1666.

THE CARTIER HALO TIARA

Kate wore the Cartier Halo Tiara on her wedding day. Queen Elizabeth II, William's grandmother, loaned the diamond tiara to Kate. It had originally been a gift from Queen Elizabeth II's father, George VI, to his wife, the Queen Mother. The Queen Mother later gave her daughter Elizabeth the tiara for her eighteenth birthday.

designer Sarah Burton of Alexander McQueen designed the dress, which had long lace sleeves and a V-shaped neckline. The lace on the bodice and skirt of the dress was handmade by the Royal School of Needlework at Hampton Court Palace. Kate wore her long hair half up and half down. Her silk tulle veil was held in place by the Cartier Halo Tiara.

Kate's younger sister, Philippa, affectionately known as Pippa, held Kate's nearly nine-foot (2.5-m) train as they climbed the steps of Westminster Abbey. Kate had chosen Pippa to serve as her maid of honor. Pippa wore a white, form-fitting gown with covered buttons down the back.

About 1,900 guests were invited to the ceremony, but millions of viewers watched the wedding as it was broadcast live to televisions across the world. Kate's father escorted her down the long center aisle of the Abbey. She smiled brightly the entire trip.

Prince William stood at the altar. He kept his back toward the aisle until she reached his side. Then he turned to admire his bride. Instead of wearing the traditional Royal Air Force uniform, William wore the uniform of the Irish Guards. Queen Elizabeth II had made this choice

MELODIES OF LOVE

Kate and William chose the music that filled the Abbey. The State Trumpeters of the Household Cavalry and the Royal Air Force Fanfare Team played the trumpet fanfares. The Choir of Westminster Abbey and the Chapel Royal Choir sang. The entire London Chamber Orchestra and the Abbey's enormous organ added to the full sound. British composer John Rutter wrote a hymn, "This Is the Day the Lord Hath Made," specifically for the day.

because she was planning an important visit to Ireland after the wedding and wanted it to start on the correct diplomatic foot. William's younger brother, Prince Harry, stood beside him.

Kate and William exchanged traditional marriage vows in the Church of England ceremony. However, Kate chose not to use the word *obey*. William's mother, Diana, Princess of Wales, had also removed the word *obey* from her wedding vows when she married William's father, Prince Charles. Instead, Kate promised to "Love, comfort, honor, and keep" her husband. William presented Kate with a wedding ring, but he chose not to wear one.

After the ceremony, the couple retreated to a private room with their parents to sign the marriage documents. This made the marriage official. Kate was now Catherine, Duchess of Cambridge. Kate and William held hands, walked down the Abbey's long aisle, and left the church. Outside, William and Kate climbed into an open carriage pulled by

Duchess Catherine and Prince William left Westminster Abbey in a horse-drawn carriage, which carried them to a reception at Buckingham Palace.

four horses. The carriage drove them through the streets past thousands of admirers. It stopped at Buckingham Palace.

Kate and William stepped out on the balcony of Buckingham Palace to wave to the crowds. They were joined by William's grandparents, Queen Elizabeth II and Prince Phillip; Prince Charles and his wife, Camilla, Duchess of Cornwall; Carole and Michael Middleton;

After the ceremony, the couple kissed on the balcony at Buckingham Palace to the cheers of an adoring crowd gathered below.

Pippa; Harry; and the children of the wedding party. The crowd went wild when William kissed Kate, not just once but twice!

There were two parties to celebrate the bride and groom. The first was a gathering at Buckingham Palace for 650 invited guests hosted by Queen Elizabeth II. That evening, Prince Charles hosted a smaller group of 300 for a reception with dinner and dancing. At the evening party, Kate wore another ivory gown designed by Sarah Burton. William and Kate danced their first dance to "Your Song" by Elton John, performed live by British singer Ellie Goulding. The night ended with a fireworks show. The guests donated money to the couple's charitable foundation instead of giving wedding gifts. The donations totaled more than $1.5 million.

Catherine was now a member of the royal family. She would make official trips to represent the Crown. Catherine would become a supporter of charities that were meaningful to her. When she became a mother, each of her children would have a place in line for the throne.

EXPLORE ONLINE

Chapter One talks about William and Kate's wedding. Visit this website to read about the event. Compare and contrast the wedding as described in this chapter with the wedding as discussed on this website. How are they different? How are they the same?

THE WEDDING OF PRINCE WILLIAM AND MISS CATHERINE MIDDLETON

abdocorelibrary.com/kate-middleton

ROYAL BERKSHIRE HOSPITAL
Disabled Access
Disabled Access

CHAPTER TWO

KATE'S EARLY YEARS

Catherine Elizabeth Middleton was born on January 9, 1982, at the Royal Berkshire Hospital in Reading, the United Kingdom. Her parents were Carole and Michael Middleton. They brought their new baby daughter home to their house in Bradfield Southend, Berkshire. They lived in a modest house that was joined to another home on one side. Kate was christened at St. Andrew's Church in Bradfield on June 20, 1982.

Kate was born at the Royal Berkshire Hospital. Years later, she and William would visit the hospital during the COVID-19 pandemic.

Kate was a commoner from a middle-class background. Her mother was a flight attendant for British Airways. Her father was a flight dispatcher at the same company. He planned when the planes took off and landed. The two met at work, fell in love, and married.

Kate came from a hardworking family. Carole's ancestors were working-class people. They had worked as coal miners and carpenters. Michael's dad was a pilot, and other family members were lawyers.

Kate's younger sister, Pippa, was born on September 6, 1983.

PARTY PIECES

While the children were young, Carole often took them to birthday parties. She also loved to plan parties and entertain. In 1987, she decided to start a home business. Carole worked at the kitchen table. She bought fun items, such as small toys, and filled party bags to sell. She called her business Party Pieces. Michael was able to quit his job at British Airways in 1989 to help with the business. Party Pieces became very successful, eventually making millions of dollars.

The girls were close in age and became good friends as they grew up. When Kate was two years old, her dad's company transferred him to Amman, Jordan. She spent two and a half years living in Jordan with her family.

When Kate was three years old, she attended Al-Saheera nursery school. The teachers taught in English and Arabic. Kate learned some nursery rhymes and how to sing "Happy Birthday" in Arabic before she learned them in English. After the Middleton family returned from Jordan in 1986, Kate started at St Andrew's Berkshire, a school in Pangbourne, the United Kingdom. Kate's brother, James, was born on April 15, 1987.

Kate studied at St Andrew's until July 1995, when she was 13 years old. While there, Kate was interested in theater. She sang and acted in the starring role of Eliza Doolittle in *My Fair Lady* when she was 11 years old. She also played the main character in *Murder in the Red Barn*. In one scene of that play, a character named William got down on one knee and asked Kate's

Kate Middleton, *front left*, played many sports during her school years. At St Andrew's School, she played rounders, a game similar to baseball.

character to marry him. She was thrilled to accept the proposal.

Kate was also a talented athlete. At St Andrew's, she played field hockey and tennis. Kate also enjoyed netball. Netball is similar to basketball, but there is no backboard, and the player does not have to dribble the ball. Kate also competed in high jumping.

HIGH SCHOOL TIME

By 1995, the Middletons moved to a larger house in the village of Bucklebury, the United Kingdom. Kate attended Downe House School near her new home.

SPORTS KATE MIDDLETON HAS PLAYED

Kate is a talented athlete who has played many sports, including field hockey, skiing, and sailing. How do you think playing sports affected Kate's school years?

Downe House was an all-girls high school. Kate faced challenges at this school. She had entered the school two years later than most of the girls, who started when they were 11. Many of the girls her age had already formed friendships. Downe House was also a boarding school, but because Kate lived nearby, she did not stay overnight. The girls who boarded spent more time with each other and formed stronger friendships. Kate was also shy. Some of the girls bullied her. Kate wasn't happy at this school, so she stayed there for only two semesters.

Kate transferred to another high school called Marlborough College. The school was in Wiltshire, a few hours from home, so she boarded there. She was much happier at this school. Kate studied hard. She became interested in photography and art. She continued to be an active athlete. Kate was captain of the field hockey team and played tennis. In her spare time, she skied and sailed. Pippa, who was also a talented athlete and student, joined her at Marlborough.

When she was in the final years of high school, Kate completed

TRAVELING IN ROYAL CIRCLES

Kate had two very close friends at Marlborough College, Emilia d'Erlanger and Alice St John Webster. These friends knew Prince William. They attended his parties and hung out with members of the royal family. It is likely that Kate had met William while she was at Marlborough, although she hasn't said so publicly.

the challenging Duke of Edinburgh Gold Award. To earn this award, she had to problem-solve and work with a team. She also became more physically fit. Her final challenge was to go on a difficult four-day hike in the wilderness.

Kate did well in her A-levels, which are advanced exams students can take after their required schooling. She earned As in both art and mathematics and a B in English. She applied and was accepted to the well-respected University of Edinburgh in Scotland.

FURTHER EVIDENCE

Chapter Two covers Kate's school years. What is the main point of this chapter? What key evidence supports this point? Go to the "Biography" section of the website below and scroll down to the "Education" heading. Find a quote from the website that supports the chapter's main point.

THE PRINCESS OF WALES

abdocorelibrary.com/kate-middleton

CHAPTER THREE

UNIVERSITY YEARS

Kate and her friends Alice St John Webster and Emilia d'Erlanger had planned to attend the University of Edinburgh in the autumn of 2000. They had even looked for places to live together near the school. However, Kate decided to take a gap year and apply to the University of St Andrews instead. In August 2000, the royal family announced that Prince William was also planning to take a gap year before attending the University of St Andrews. The media and

After taking a gap year, Kate enrolled at the University of St Andrews in Scotland.

At St Andrews, Kate lived in St Salvator's Hall, the same dormitory where Prince William lived.

others have speculated about whether William's plans had influenced Kate's choice.

Kate began her gap year by attending the British Institute of Florence in Italy. There, she studied art and the Italian language. In January 2001, Kate traveled to Chile with the UK expedition and charity company Raleigh International. She spent her first three weeks in the program walking far into Chile as a wilderness survival exercise. The next three weeks, she traveled in an inflatable boat to help scientists study marine life. For the last part of her stay, Kate helped build a new fire station. Prince William also participated in the Raleigh International program in Chile during his gap year. But he was there at a different time.

To complete the gap year, Kate worked on the crew of Round the World Challenge boats in the Solent. The Solent is a body of water separating the Isle of Wight from Great Britain.

ST ANDREWS

Kate was accepted to the University of St Andrews in Scotland. She chose to study history of art and began in 2001. She played field hockey on the St Andrews team. Prince William also started at St Andrews in 2001 and studied history of art.

Kate and William both lived in St Salvator's Hall. They shared some of the same classes. If William missed a class, Kate would bring him notes. Kate and William often ate breakfast together with a group of friends. They both enjoyed sports, and they swam together. The two became friends.

Despite his growing friendship with Kate, William was unhappy during his first term at the university. He nearly quit over the holiday break, but his father, Prince Charles, convinced him to stay. William returned, but he changed his major from art history to geography. That spring, William asked Kate to be his flatmate for their second year at the university. They would live off campus with two other friends, Olivia Bleasdale and Fergus Boyd.

In March 2002, Kate participated in Don't Walk. This was a charity fashion show to raise money for the victims of the September 11, 2001, terrorist attack in the United States.

TRUST IS A MUST

Prince William was very careful about whom he chose as friends. He needed to be able to trust those close to him. He wanted to make sure they would not share stories with the press. Sometimes he tested new people in his life by telling them a lie. If that lie was reported in the press, he knew the person could not be trusted. Kate was a friend who could be trusted.

Kate walked down the runway in a see-through dress. The sheer piece was designed by Charlotte Todd.

THE KATE EFFECT

Kate is known for her stylish fashion sense. Her style has been called a mix of dressed up and sporty. She often wears UK designers' clothing. When she wears something affordable, the public buys it quickly, and it often sells out. This is known as the Kate Effect.

William attended the fashion show. When he saw Kate modeling on the runway, he began to think of her as more than just a friend. William tried to kiss Kate that night. But she was dating a fourth-year law student named Rupert Finch, so Kate turned him down. But over the following year, things changed. While William and Kate were flatmates, they also became a couple. They were private about their relationship.

In their third year at the university, William and Kate moved to Balgove House, a farmhouse farther

Kate joined the royal family on a ski trip to the Swiss Alps in 2004.

from school. They shared the home with friends Oliver Baker and Alasdair Coutts-Wood.

Kate and William's romance became public in March 2004 when they took a ski trip to the Swiss Alps. Photographers caught William kissing Kate, and the media published the photos.

Kate graduated from the University of St Andrews on June 23, 2005, with a degree in the History of Art. Her proud parents shared the day with her. William also graduated that day with a degree in geography. His father, stepmother, and grandparents came to see him accept his diploma.

STRAIGHT TO THE SOURCE

Kate, William, and many members of the royal family hunt. They hunt deer and game birds, among other animals. In the following quotation, the British Deer Society defends deer hunting as a way to benefit the environment:

> *Deer are an important part of the UK's countryside ecology and have a vital role to play in creating balanced ecosystems. However, deer numbers are thought to be higher than at any time in the last 1,000 years, and in some areas of the UK they have reached levels where they may have a [harmful] effect on habitats that they and other species depend on. . . .*
>
> *We accept that there is a requirement for the careful management of deer.*

Source: "British Deer Society Position Statement." *British Deer Society*, n.d., bds.org.uk. Accessed 14 May 2024.

BACK IT UP

The author of this passage is using evidence to support a point. Write a paragraph describing the point the author is making. Then write down the pieces of evidence used to support that point.

CHAPTER FOUR

THE ROAD TO BEING ROYAL

After Kate's graduation from St Andrews, she and William continued to see each other. William went to Army officer training at the Royal Military Academy at Sandhurst. He became an officer in the Household Cavalry. He would later train as a search and rescue pilot for the Royal Air Force. William learned to fly both planes and helicopters.

While William was training for the military, Kate was testing the career waters. She was interested in fashion. She began a children's

With a history of art degree from St Andrews in hand, Kate set out to begin her career.

clothing business as part of her parents' Party Pieces company. She chose fabrics and designed clothes. But the business wasn't successful, and in 2006, Kate left Party Pieces. She had landed a job as a clothing accessory buyer at Jigsaw, a clothing business. Close friends of her family owned the company. There, she worked a four-day week. She wanted to have a flexible schedule so she could spend time with William. Kate worked at Jigsaw for one year before leaving to try something new.

In April 2007, Kate drew on her passion for photography. She organized an exhibit of

HOLD STILL

Kate's art history background made her a perfect fit as patron of the National Portrait Gallery. In 2020, Kate launched the project *Hold Still*. For this project, Kate invited people to submit photographs of their time during the COVID-19 pandemic. Judges chose 100 photos to be used in a public digital exhibit. They were also published in a book. The money from the book sales was split between the National Portrait Gallery and the mental health charity Mind.

photographs by Alistair Morrison, who takes portraits of celebrities. The exhibit raised money for the United Nations Children's Fund (UNICEF). Later, Kate returned to work at Party Pieces. She took photographs for the website.

RELATIONSHIP UPS AND DOWNS

Kate dated William for six years after they graduated from St Andrews. He had told the press that he didn't plan to marry until he was close to 30 years old. Meanwhile, Kate spent much of her time traveling and socializing. She loved to visit the exclusive Caribbean island Mustique. She also visited expensive ski resorts. The press gave her the nickname "Waity Katie," because she seemed to be passing time until William was ready to marry.

The Queen was reportedly concerned about Kate's lack of career and work ethic. To be a working member of the royal family means many hours of effort representing the Crown.

Kate trained with The Sisterhood rowing team on the Thames River in August 2007.

Then, in April 2007, the media published information about William flirting with other women at bars. William and Kate broke up. She was looking for a long-term commitment from him that he didn't seem ready to offer.

After the breakup, Kate went with her mother to Ireland. Her mother offered support and advice. After her return, Kate joined The Sisterhood. This was a women's rowing team that was planning to row across the English Channel for charity. Kate trained with them for a few months. By July 1, 2007, William and Kate had made up and were back together.

In October 2010, Kate and William went on a safari in Kenya. They were staying at a remote log cabin at Rutundu on Mount Kenya when William proposed. Kate found the proposal romantic.

William offered her his mother's engagement ring, which featured a sapphire surrounded by diamonds. William's mother, Princess Diana, had been killed in a car accident when William was 15. William said that this way, his mother could be part of it all. Prince Charles announced Prince William and Kate's engagement to the press on November 16, 2010.

A WORKING ROYAL

After the couple's grand wedding at Westminster Abbey in April 2011, Kate's married life began. She had also become a working member of the royal family. As such, she was expected to travel all over the world representing the Crown. She met with leaders and citizens of other countries. Kate's first official trip as a royal was to Canada with William in July 2011.

Kate, *second from right*, wore one of her signature hats to attend the Trooping the Colour event in June 2012.

She also attended official functions such as Trooping the Colour, a celebration that marks the king or queen's birthday.

As part of her work, Kate also supported many charities. Organizations that help children were near to her heart. Since before she was married, Kate had supported children's hospices. She became the patron of East Anglia's Children's Hospice. These are programs

that care for people who are dying. She advocated for children's mental health. She also championed the importance of early childhood development. And she began the Royal Foundation for Early Childhood. Kate also believed that children need to be active and spend time outdoors. As an athlete herself, she knew that exercise is good for physical and mental health. Kate even acted as an Olympic ambassador of the

FAMILY HOMES

Kate, William, and their children have many houses. In 2024, Adelaide Cottage served as the main family home. Would you prefer to have just one home or more than one home? Explain your answer.

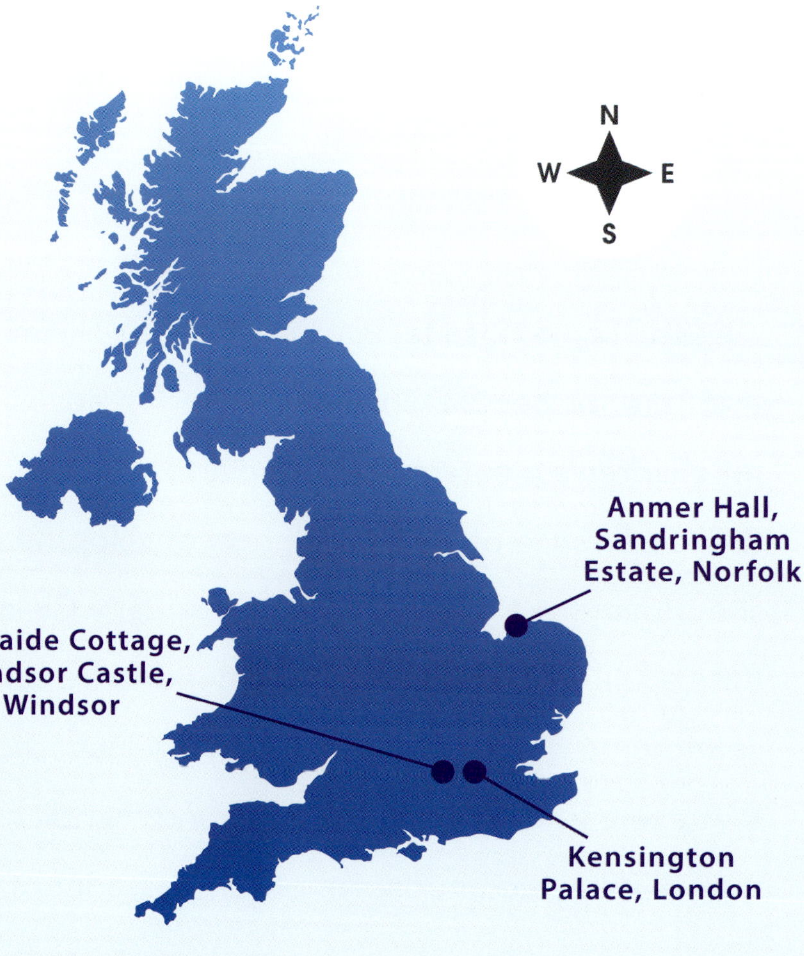

United Kingdom's Olympic and Paralympic teams for the 2012 Olympic Games in London.

RAISING A FAMILY

In December 2012, the royal family announced that Kate was pregnant. This was not an easy time for Kate. She suffered with hyperemesis gravidarum, which is severe morning sickness. She was so ill that she had to spend time in the hospital. But Kate delivered a healthy baby boy. Kate and William's first child, Prince George, was born on July 22, 2013, in St Mary's Hospital. This was the same hospital in which Prince William had been born. As William's firstborn son, Prince George is heir to the throne. This means he will one day be king of the United Kingdom.

Kate and William had two more children. Princess Charlotte was born on May 2, 2015. Prince Louis was born on April 23, 2018. Kate was very involved in her children's lives. She took them to school and organized play dates and other activities. They went to the beach

Kate and William visit Lambrook School with their children, *from left to right*, Prince George, Prince Louis, and Princess Charlotte.

to build sandcastles. They went on bike rides. Kate and William expected their children to do chores. William was also an involved dad. When the children were young, he helped with baths and read them bedtime stories.

When Queen Elizabeth II died on September 8, 2022, King Charles III ascended to the throne. This meant William, Prince of Wales, became next in line for the throne. Kate became Catherine, Princess of Wales.

ROYAL WOMEN'S RIGHTS

For centuries in royal families, a younger son had the right to ascend to the throne before his older sister. In April 2013, Parliament changed the law to say that either the firstborn son or firstborn daughter could ascend to the throne. The new law is called the Succession to the Crown Act.

STARTLING NEWS

In January 2024, Kate and William learned that Kate needed abdominal surgery. The royal family announced that she would step back from official duties until Easter of 2024. This would give her time to recover. But the public became concerned when an edited photo of Kate and her children was posted on social media. People wondered what was happening behind the scenes.

On March 22, 2024, the royal family released a video. In it, Kate revealed that she had cancer.

Catherine, Princess of Wales, presented the winner's trophy to Carlos Alcaraz of Spain at the 2024 Wimbledon Championships in July.

She explained that doctors were treating her with chemotherapy. She hoped to make a full recovery and return to work as soon as possible. After her announcement, people were quick to wish her well.

Kate has led a remarkable life so far. She has a busy life as a mother of three and a working member of the royal family. The world looks forward to Kate's future contributions.

STRAIGHT TO THE SOURCE

In a video statement released on March 22, 2024, Kate talked about her cancer diagnosis:

> *In January, I underwent major abdominal surgery in London and at the time, it was thought that my condition was non-cancerous. The surgery was successful. However, tests after the operation found cancer had been present. My medical team therefore advised that I should undergo a course of preventative chemotherapy and I am now in the early stages of that treatment. . . . My work has always brought me a deep sense of joy and I look forward to being back when I am able, but for now I must focus on making a full recovery.*

Source: "Kate Middleton Announces She Has Cancer in a Video Message." *YouTube*, uploaded by AP, 22 Mar. 2024, youtube.com. Accessed 11 Apr. 2024.

WHAT'S THE BIG IDEA?

Read this passage carefully. What is its main idea? How did Kate discover she had cancer? What treatment was she undergoing? Was she hopeful about regaining her health?

IMPORTANT DATES

January 9, 1982
Catherine Elizabeth Middleton is born at Royal Berkshire Hospital in Reading, United Kingdom.

1995
Kate attends Downe House School. After two semesters, she transfers to Marlborough College.

2000–2001
Kate takes a gap year, traveling to Italy and Chile before starting at University of St Andrews.

June 23, 2005
Kate graduates from the University of St Andrews.

November 16, 2010
Kate and William's engagement is officially announced.

April 29, 2011
Kate and William marry at Westminster Abbey.

July 22, 2013
Kate's son George is born.

May 2, 2015
Kate's daughter Charlotte is born.

April 23, 2018
Kate's son Louis is born.

March 2024
Kate announces her cancer diagnosis.

STOP AND THINK

Surprise Me

Chapter Two discusses Kate Middleton's childhood. After reading this chapter, what two or three facts about her childhood did you find most surprising? Write a few sentences about each fact. Why did you find each fact surprising?

Say What?

Reading about Kate Middleton and her life in the United Kingdom means learning a lot of new vocabulary. Find five words in this book that you've never heard before. Use a dictionary to find out what they mean.

Take a Stand

Chapter Four discusses some criticism of Kate Middleton's difficulty finding and keeping a job when she was dating William. Do you think it is important to have a good work ethic? Why?

Why Do I Care?

Chapter Two says that Kate Middleton was bullied by her schoolmates at Downe House School. What could you do if a friend of yours was being bullied? What would you do if you were the target of a bully? Who would you turn to for help? What steps could you take to protect yourself from being bullied?

GLOSSARY

ascend
to take the throne as king or queen

chemotherapy
the use of chemicals to treat disease

christen
to ceremonially welcome a person into the church

commoner
a person without a royal title or rank

diplomatic
concerned with the art of negotiating between nations

flatmate
a person who shares an apartment

Household Cavalry
the senior regiments of the British Army

patron
a person who gives support to an organization

safari
an expedition to hunt or observe animals in their natural habitat

succession
the order in which the royal family members stand in line to the throne

train
extra fabric that extends from the back of a gown and trails behind

ONLINE RESOURCES

To learn more about Kate Middleton, visit our free resource websites below.

Core Library CONNECTION
FREE! COMMON CORE MULTIMEDIA RESOURCES

Visit **abdocorelibrary.com** or scan this QR code for free Common Core resources for teachers and students, including vetted activities, multimedia, and booklinks, for deeper subject comprehension.

Booklinks NONFICTION NETWORK
FREE! ONLINE NONFICTION RESOURCES

Visit **abdobooklinks.com** or scan this QR code for free additional online weblinks for further learning. These links are routinely monitored and updated to provide the most current information available.

LEARN MORE

Gagne, Tammy. *Charles III*. Abdo, 2025.

Grodzicki, Jenna. *The Story of Princess Diana*. Rockridge, 2021.

Stine, Megan. *Who Is Queen Elizabeth II?* Penguin Workshop, 2021.

INDEX

About the Author

Marie-Therese Miller is an award-winning author of more than 45 nonfiction books for children and teens. Miller earned her PhD in English from St. John's University. She teaches Children's and YA Literature at Marist College. Miller and her husband have five grown children and a grandson.